P·I·C·T·U·R·E·P·E·D·I·A

NOTE TO PARENTS

This book is part of PICTUREPEDIA, a completely
new kind of information series for children.
Its unique combination of pictures and words
encourages children to use their eyes to discover and
explore the world, while introducing them to a wealth
of basic knowledge. Clear, straightforward text
explains each picture thoroughly and provides
additional information about the topic.

'Looking it up' becomes an easy task with
PICTUREPEDIA, an ideal first reference for all types of
schoolwork. Because PICTUREPEDIA is also entertaining,
children will enjoy reading its words and looking
at its pictures over and over again. You can encourage
and stimulate further inquiry by helping your child
pose simple questions for the whole family to
'look up' and answer together.

The EARTH

DORLING KINDERSLEY

LONDON, NEW YORK, AUCKLAND
DELHI, MUNICH, SYDNEY

DK www.dk.com

First published in Great Britain in 1992
by Dorling Kindersley Limited, London

This updated edition published in 2000 by:

Dorling Kindersley Limited
9 Henrietta Street, London WC2E 8PS, Great Britain

Dorling Kindersley Publishing Pty Limited
(A.C.N. 078 414 445)
118-120 Pacific Highway, St Leonards NSW 2065, Australia

Dorling Kindersley (India) Pvt. Ltd.
102/3 Kaushalya Park, Hauz Khas, New Delhi 110016, India

A CIP catalogue record for this
book is available from the British Library.

ISBN 0 7513 6901 2

Reproduction by Colourscan, Singapore
Printed and bound by L. Rex Printing Company Limited, China

The EARTH

DK

A DORLING KINDERSLEY BOOK

CONTENTS

THE EARTH IN SPACE 6

A VIEW FROM SPACE 8

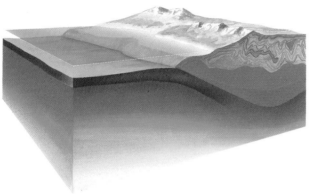
THE EARTH'S CRUST 10

MOVING PLATES 12
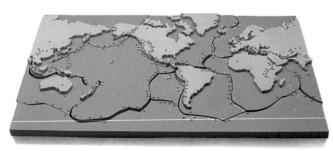

VOLCANOES 14

EARTHQUAKES 16

ROCKS 18

MINERALS 20

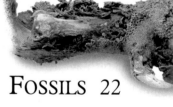
FOSSILS 22

CAVES 24

OCEANS 26

COASTLINES 28

CLIMATE 38

CLOUDS 40

GLACIERS 30

THUNDER AND
LIGHTNING 42

RIVERS 32

WIND 44

DESERTS 34

TAKING CARE OF THE EARTH 46

THE ATMOSPHERE 36

GLOSSARY &
INDEX 48

THE EARTH IN SPACE

To us, planet Earth seems enormous, but in the vastness of space it is only a tiny speck. It is one of the nine planets that hurtle continuously around a star – our Sun – in huge paths called orbits. Together, Sun and planets are called the solar system. This, in turn, is part of a galaxy, one of the 6,000 million known ones that make up the universe.

Star Bright
The solar system belongs to a cluster of millions of stars and planets called a galaxy. Our galaxy is spiral shaped and is called the Milky Way. It is so vast that a jet would take 100 billion years to fly across it.

A comet looks like a star with a long tail.

Asteroids

Mars

The Moon

Taking Measurements
All the planets are different sizes. They are shown here in proportion to one another. Can you tell which is the largest planet and which is the smallest? Two of the planets are very similar in size. Can you pick out which ones they are?

Earth

Venus

Mercury

THE SUN

Different Worlds
The Moon orbits the Earth. It is the Earth's satellite and neighbour but it is totally lifeless. Humans first walked on the Moon in 1969.

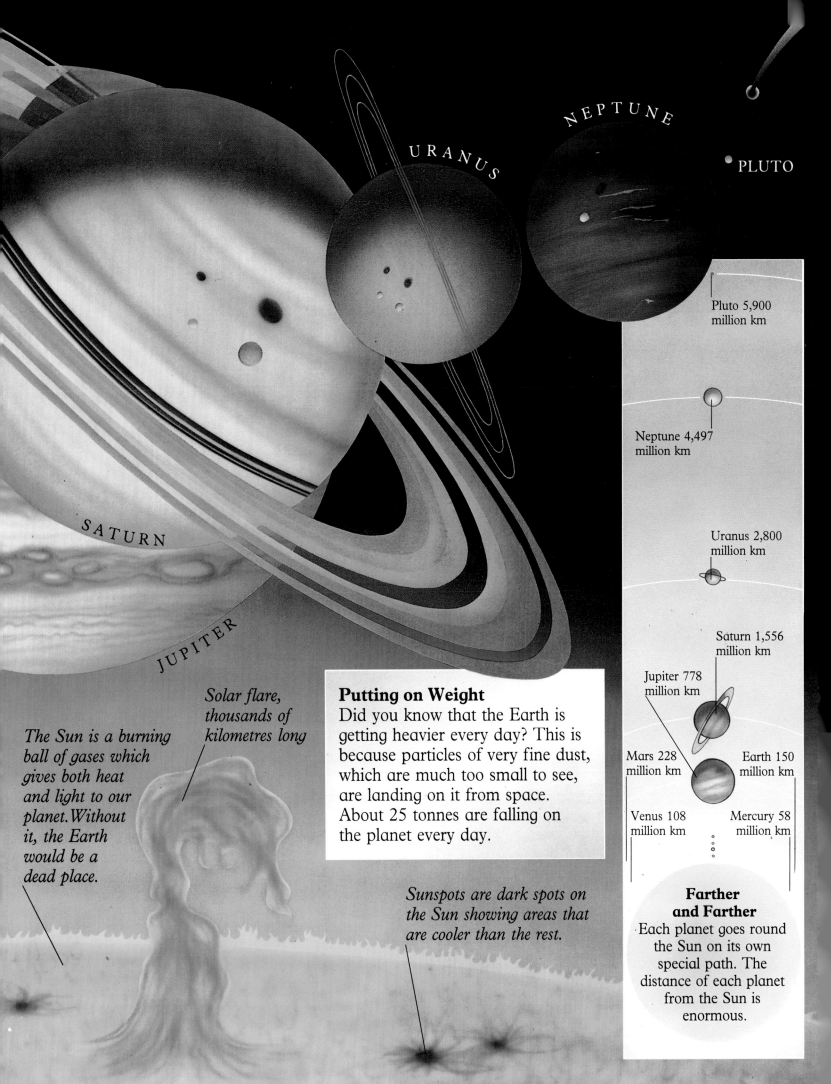

NEPTUNE

URANUS

PLUTO

SATURN

JUPITER

Pluto 5,900
million km

Neptune 4,497
million km

Uranus 2,800
million km

Saturn 1,556
million km

Jupiter 778
million km

Mars 228
million km

Earth 150
million km

Venus 108
million km

Mercury 58
million km

Solar flare,
thousands of
kilometres long

The Sun is a burning
ball of gases which
gives both heat
and light to our
planet. Without
it, the Earth
would be a
dead place.

Putting on Weight
Did you know that the Earth is
getting heavier every day? This is
because particles of very fine dust,
which are much too small to see,
are landing on it from space.
About 25 tonnes are falling on
the planet every day.

Sunspots are dark spots on
the Sun showing areas that
are cooler than the rest.

**Farther
and Farther**
Each planet goes round
the Sun on its own
special path. The
distance of each planet
from the Sun is
enormous.

7

A VIEW FROM SPACE

Imagine you are an astronaut in space looking at the Earth through the porthole of your spacecraft. You see a big, blue ball that is always covered by swirling, white clouds. The clouds make it hard for you to see the Earth in detail, but if they were not there, you would be able to see land and mountains, sea, ice and rivers.

Homing In
Even small features can be seen from space. This photo shows London, UK, in detail.

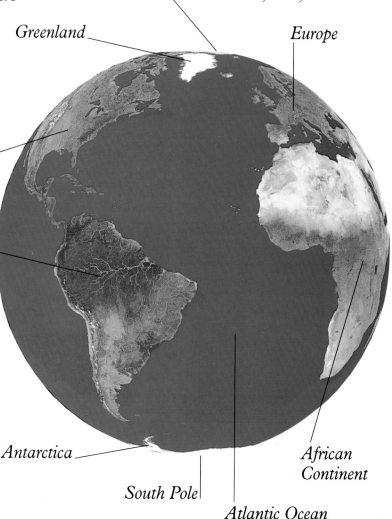

North Pole

Greenland

Europe

North American Continent

South American Continent

Antarctica

South Pole

Atlantic Ocean

African Continent

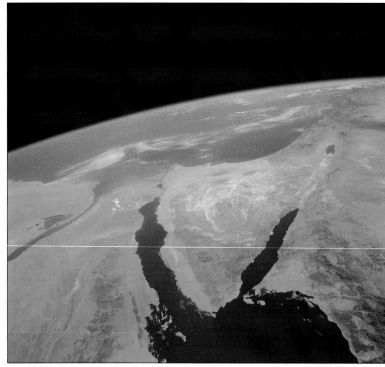

Grand Scale
Parts of Egypt, Israel, Jordan and Saudi Arabia are shown in this photo. You can see the Mediterranean Sea at the top and the northern part of the Red Sea at the bottom.

Why is the Earth Blue?
The Earth looks blue from space because more than two thirds of it is made up of huge oceans and smaller seas. From some places in space, you would see nearly all water and only a tiny amount of land.

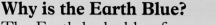

Viewpoint

If you had been one of the crew of the space shuttle Columbia 6, this is how you would have seen the Himalayas as you circled the Earth.

Panorama

From space, you are looking at the area in Japan which contains Tokyo.

Himalayas

Middle East

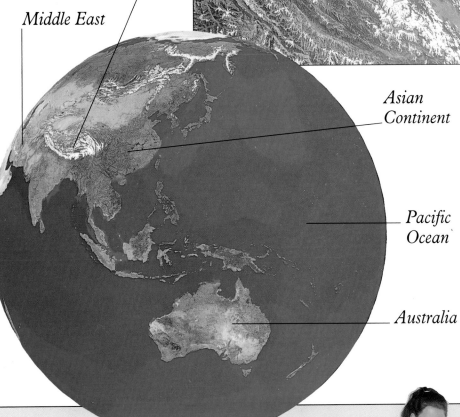

Asian Continent

Pacific Ocean

Australia

Lighting Up the Sky

At night, the lights of cities show you where lots of people live. The black patches show deserts and mountains, which are mostly uninhabited, and oceans.

How Maps are Made

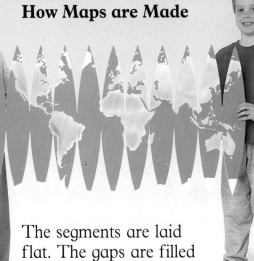

The Earth is round, like a ball. When a map is made, it is shown flat.

The best way to flatten out the Earth is to split it into pieces, like the segments of an orange.

The segments are laid flat. The gaps are filled in to make the map whole and an oblong shape.

THE EARTH'S CRUST

Just like you, the Earth has a very delicate skin. It is so thin that if you compare it to the whole Earth, it is thinner than the skin of an apple.

The Earth's skin, or crust, is made up of rock, built up in layers over millions of years. The layers look like blankets on a bed, with lots of lumps and bumps in them.

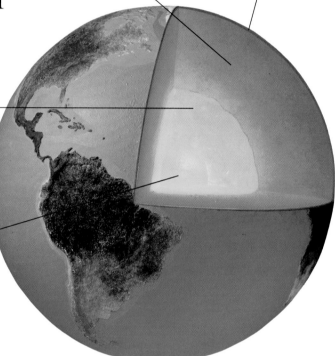

The crust is a thin layer of rock between 6 and 70 kilometres thick.

The mantle is the layer below the crust. In parts of it, the rock has melted like treacle.

The outer core is made of iron and nickel that has melted to form a liquid.

The inner core is a ball of iron and nickel. It is hotter here than at the outer core, but the ball stays solid because of the enormous pressure.

How Mountains are Made

Mountains are made when the Earth's crust is pushed up in big folds or forced up or down in blocks. The different shapes made are given different names.

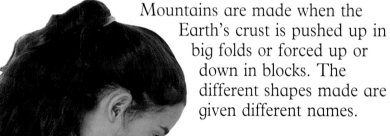

Overfold

Downfold

Upfold

The sea lies on top of the oceanic crust. The oceanic crust also runs underneath the continental crust.

The land is made out of the continental crust. It is thickest where mountains are found.

Under the oceans the crust is as little as 6 kilometres thick, but under the continents it is up to 70 kilometres thick.

The mantle

Block mountain

Fault

Rift valley

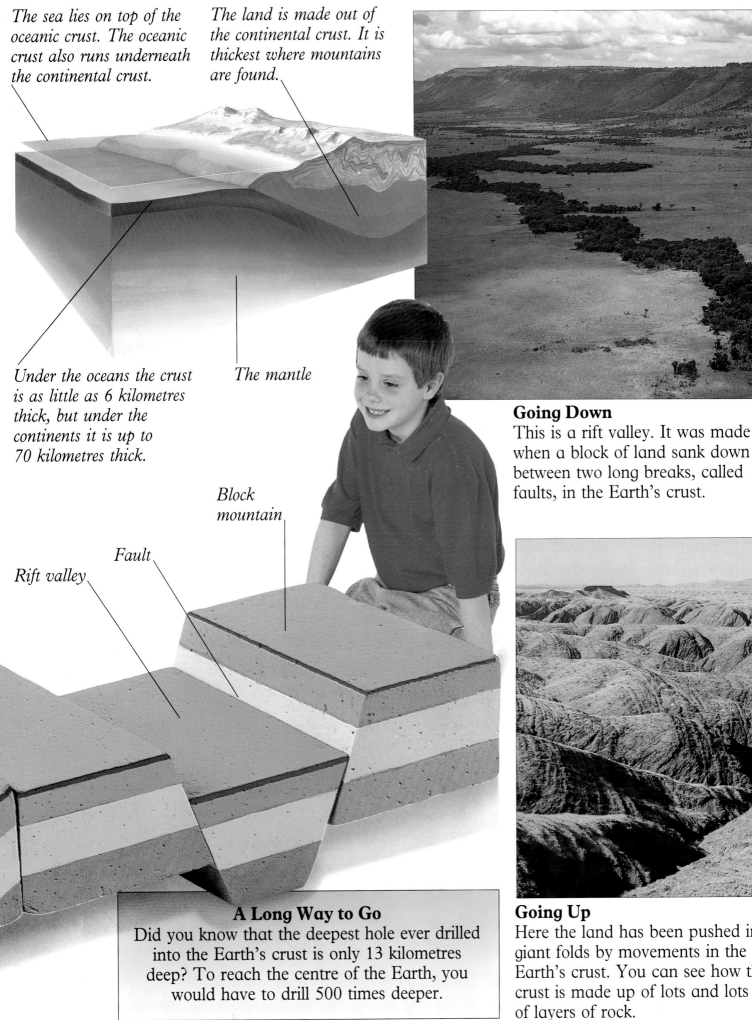

Going Down
This is a rift valley. It was made when a block of land sank down between two long breaks, called faults, in the Earth's crust.

A Long Way to Go
Did you know that the deepest hole ever drilled into the Earth's crust is only 13 kilometres deep? To reach the centre of the Earth, you would have to drill 500 times deeper.

Going Up
Here the land has been pushed into giant folds by movements in the Earth's crust. You can see how the crust is made up of lots and lots of layers of rock.

MOVING PLATES

The Earth's crust is not one unbroken piece. It is made up of many pieces that fit together like a giant jigsaw puzzle. These pieces, called plates, ride on soft, partly melted rock moving underneath them. The pieces push against each other with spectacular effects – earthquakes split the crust, volcanoes form, new land is made and huge mountain ranges are pushed skywards.

All Scrunched Up
Sometimes, two plates push against each other and then crumple the land to make huge mountain ranges.

Going Down
Sometimes, one plate slides under another. It is pushed down into the mantle and melts.

Doing the Splits
Sometimes, two plates split apart and lava bubbles up to fill the gap. It hardens and makes new land.

Slip, Sliding Away
Sometimes, two plates slip sideways past each other. This kind of movement causes earthquakes.

The red dots show you the places where volcanoes erupt.

Continent

On the Move
The plates are never still, they are always moving. In one year they can move about 2.5 centimetres, about as much as your fingernails grow in the same amount of time.

Past, Present, Future

Have you ever wondered what the Earth looked like in the past? These pictures show you how the continents have moved over the last 300 million years, and how the world may look 50 million years from now.

300 MILLION YEARS AGO

Changing Places

The land is coming together to make one gigantic continent.

200 MILLION YEARS AGO

PANGAEA

All Together

The super continent has come together. It is called Pangaea.

150 MILLION YEARS AGO

LAURASIA

GONDWANALAND

Worlds Apart

The land is drifting apart again. Pangaea is splitting into two, Laurasia and Gondwanaland.

The Restless Earth

These houses and roads in Iceland are near a spot where two plates meet and have split the land.

The green dots show you the places where earthquakes happen.

This is where two plates meet.

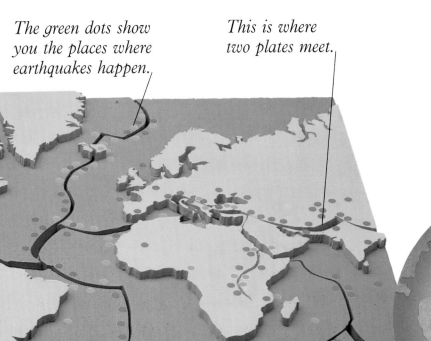

TODAY

Familiar Ground

Today, the world looks like this, but the continents are still moving.

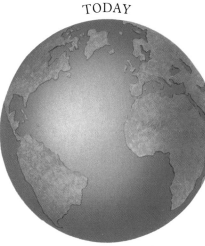

50 MILLION YEARS TIME

Looking Ahead

This is how the world may look in 50 million years' time. Can you spot how the land has changed its shape? To start you off, find Africa on the globe and see how it has joined up with Europe.

VOLCANOES

When you shake up a can of fizzy drink and then pull off the tab, the contents shoot out with a great whoosh! A volcano acts a bit like this. With tremendous force, molten rock bursts through weak parts in the Earth's crust and is hurled high into the sky.

Volcanoes can be quiet and not erupt for a long time.

Hot springs are often found near volcanoes.

Nature's Fireworks
This volcano is putting on its own spectacular fireworks display. The explosions of red-hot lava and ash from the crater look like gigantic 'Roman candles'.

The Spotter's Guide to Volcano Shapes

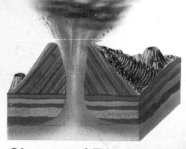

Spreading Out
Some volcanoes are flat. Their lava is very runny, so it spreads out in a thin sheet.

Short and Plump
Some volcanoes are dumpy. They are made of ash, which is lava that has turned to dust.

Going Up
Some volcanoes have pointed cones. Their lava is thick and sticky so it does not run far.

River of Fire

The red-hot molten rock that is streaming down the sides of this volcano is beautiful but deadly. It is so hot that it can melt steel.

Clouds of ash and gas pour out from the crater.

Molten rock, called magma, rises up the main pipe and any branch pipes.

A volcano builds up from layers of ash and lava.

Branch pipe

Mixed Bunch

When lava cools and hardens, it can make rocks with different shapes. Here are three types:

Runny lava

Ropy lava

A volcanic 'bomb'

Magma collects in a chamber found deep underground. It is forced up through cracks and holes in the ground.

EARTHQUAKES

Our planet is a restless place. Every 30 seconds, somewhere on Earth the ground suddenly rumbles and trembles. Most of the movements are so slight that they are not felt. Others bring complete disaster. Big cracks appear in the land, streets buckle and buildings crumble. Whole towns and cities can be destroyed. Then everything settles down but is totally changed. An earthquake has left its mark.

Fires are started by broken gas pipes and broken electrical cables.

Telephone lines brought down

Cars are smashed and they settle at crazy angles.

Unsafe Ground
This is the San Andreas Fault in California, USA. Earthquakes regularly happen here.

Terror from the Sea
Earthquakes under the sea can cause long, giant, destructive waves called *tsunamis*.

On this side of the fault the land has moved towards you.

An earthquake occurs along a fault in the seabed.

Tsunamis can travel many kilometres across the ocean.

Why Earthquakes Happen

You may think that your feet are firmly on the ground, but the Earth's crust is moving all the time. It is made of moving parts called plates. When the plates slide past or into each other, the rocks jolt and send out shock waves.

Shaken Up

The Mercalli Scale measures how much the surface of the Earth shakes during an earthquake. There are 12 intensities, or grades. At intensity 1, the effects are not felt, but by intensity 12, the shock waves can be seen and there is total destruction.

What to do in an Earthquake

Indoors, lie down under a bed or heavy table, or stand in a doorway or a corner of a room. After a minute, when the tremors will usually have finished, go outside, away from buildings, to a wide-open space.

Fault line

On this side of the fault the land has moved away from you.

Earthquake Words

The place within the Earth where an earthquake starts is called the focus. The earthquake is usually strongest at the epicentre. This is the point on the Earth's surface directly above the focus. The study of earthquakes and the shock waves they send out is called seismology.

Destructive Force

A *tsunami* piles up and gets very tall before it crashes onto the shore. It is so powerful that it can smash harbours and towns and sweep ships inland.

A *tsunami* can be more than 60 metres high and can travel as fast as a jet.

ROCKS

Movements in the Earth's crust are slowly changing the rocks that make up the surface of our planet. Mountains are pushed up and weathered away, and the fragments moved and made into other rocks. These rocks may be dragged down into the mantle and melted by its fierce heat. When a volcano erupts, the melted rock is thrown to the surface as lava, which cools and hardens as rock. This is broken down by weathering, and so the cycle starts again.

Limestone

Conglomerate

Sedimentary Rocks
These are made from bits of rock and plant and animal remains. They are broken into fine pieces and carried by rivers into the sea. They pile up in layers and press together to make solid rock. The Painted Desert, in Arizona, USA, is made of sedimentary rocks.

Red sandstone

In the Beginning
Rocks belong to three basic types. Igneous rocks are made from magma or lava and are also known as 'fiery' rocks. Sedimentary rocks are made in layers from broken rocks. Metamorphic rocks can start off as any type. They are changed by heat and weight and are called 'changed form' rocks.

In time, material moved by rivers and piled up in the sea will become sedimentary rocks.

Rock fragments are carried from one place to another by rivers, glaciers, the wind and the sea.

Recently formed sedimentary rocks

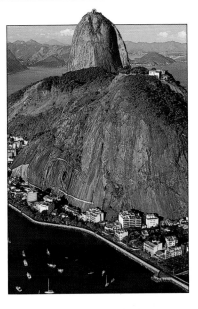

Igneous Rocks

These are made from magma or lava. It cools and hardens inside the Earth's crust or on the surface when it erupts from a volcano. Sugar Loaf Mountain, Brazil, was once igneous rock under the crust. The rocks above and around it have been worn away.

Metamorphic Rocks

These are igneous or sedimentary rocks that are changed by underground heat, underground weight, or both. This marble was once limestone, a sedimentary rock. It was changed into marble by intense heat.

Marble

Slate

Obsidian

Granite

Some rocks are thrust up as mountain ranges when the crust moves and makes giant folds.

Volcano

Surface rocks are broken down by the weather and by the scraping effect of tiny pieces of rock carried in the wind or in the ice of glaciers.

Glacier

Molten rock that cools and hardens inside the Earth is called intrusive igneous rock.

Lava that erupts from a volcano forms extrusive igneous rock.

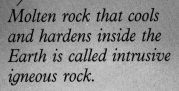

Metamorphic rocks

Folded rocks

Magma

MINERALS

Every time you put rock salt on your food, use a pencil, sprinkle yourself with talcum powder, or tell the time by a quartz watch, you are using minerals. Minerals make up rocks, but we adapt them to make all sorts of things that we use in our everyday lives.

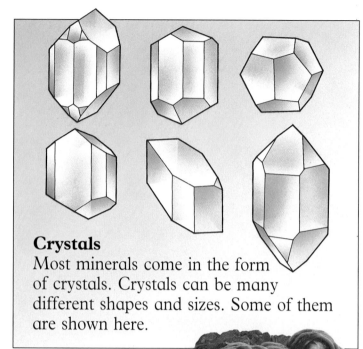

Crystals
Most minerals come in the form of crystals. Crystals can be many different shapes and sizes. Some of them are shown here.

Quartz

Ores
Minerals that contain metals are known as ores. Hematite is an important iron ore which is used to make steel.

Hematite, an iron ore.

A steel screw

Rock Builders
Minerals are the building blocks of rocks. Some rocks are made up of only one mineral, others contain many of them. If you look at granite, for example, you will see that it is made of quartz, feldspars and mica.

Feldspar

Mica

Mercury ore

Liquid Rock
Did you know that the liquid mercury inside a thermometer was once hard? Mercury ore is a rock, but mercury itself is a liquid at normal temperatures.

Granite

Mercury thermometer

Hard, Harder, Hardest
Some minerals are soft, some are hard. This scale of hardness goes up in ten steps, starting with the softest mineral, talc, and ending with the hardest, diamond. It is called the Mohs scale after the person who invented it in 1812.

①
Talc

②
Gypsum

③
Calcite

④
Fluorite

⑤
Apatite

⑥
Orthoclase

Beautiful and Rare

Gold and silver are precious metals that are found in rocks. They are prized for their beauty and rarity and both of them are used to make jewellery.

Veins of gold in quartz

Silver

The Cutting Edge

Rough diamonds look like small pebbles of cloudy glass. Their sparkle and shine show only when they have been cut and polished.

On the Mend

The plaster used to set a broken limb is made from a mineral which is called gypsum.

Gems

Gems are rare and precious minerals that are mainly used to make jewellery. Diamonds, emeralds, rubies, sapphires and opals are all well-known, valuable gems, but many lesser-known minerals are also used.

Sapphire and diamonds

Lapis lazuli

Carnelian

Onyx

Turquoise

Gold

Silver

Malachite

Blue agate

Smoky quartz

Quartz watch

7

8

9

10

Quartz

Topaz

Corundum

Diamond

21

FOSSILS

Imagine you are a detective who wants to find out what life on Earth was like millions of years ago. You look for clues and discover that the best ones are fossils. Fossils are the remains or evidence of animals and plants saved in stone, peat, ice or tar. They may be as large as a dinosaur skeleton or as small as a grain of pollen that can be seen only under a microscope.

Reading the Signs
The *Allosaurus* hunted other dinosaurs for food. Because there are two sets of footprints following one another, the *Allosaurus* may have been tracking the *Apatosaurus* to kill it and eat it.

Allosaurus

Fossil in the Making
A dead animal may be covered with sand or mud in a lake, river or sea, or on land.

The sand or mud hardens into rock. The bones of the animal are preserved in the rock as a fossil.

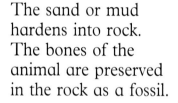

The rock is folded and pushed up. Wind and rain wear away the top layers.

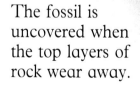

The fossil is uncovered when the top layers of rock wear away.

Back from the Past
When Vesuvius erupted over Pompeii, this dog's body left a hollow in the ash that hardened around it. When plaster was poured into the hollow, the dog's shape was recreated.

Birdlike tracks from the dinosaur called Allosaurus

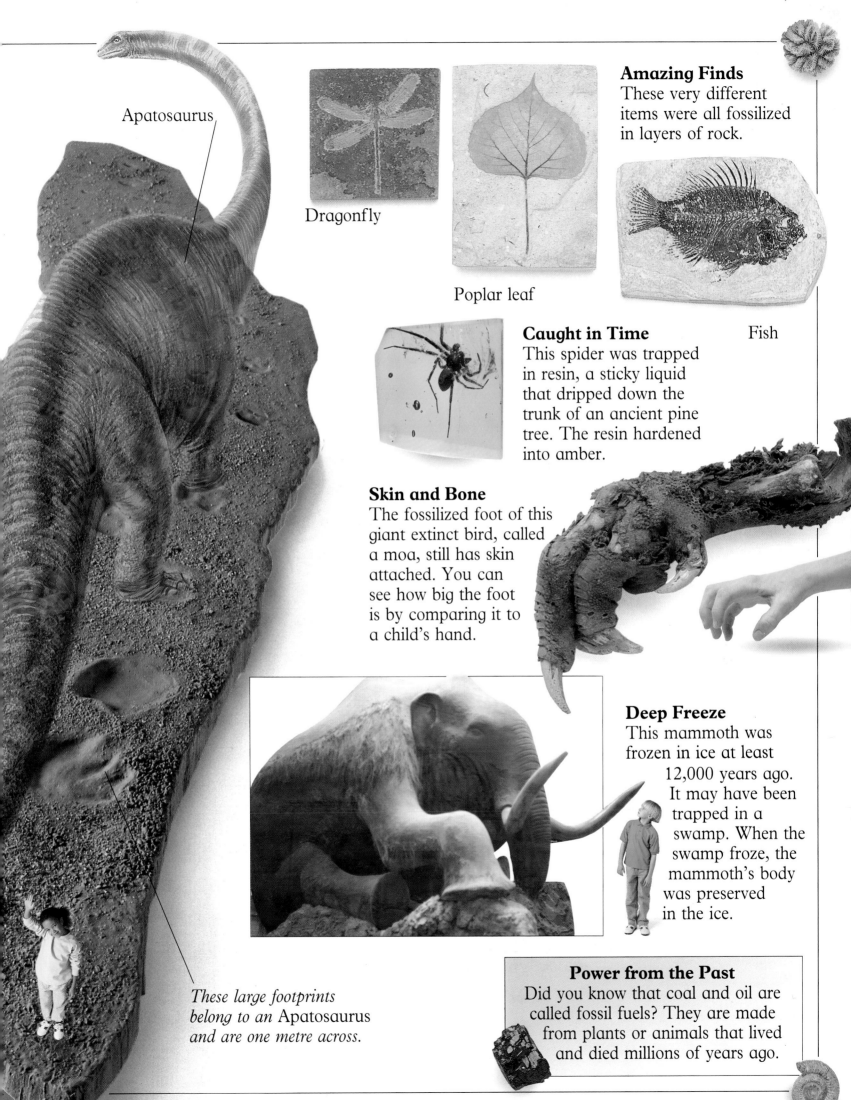

Apatosaurus

Dragonfly

Poplar leaf

Amazing Finds
These very different items were all fossilized in layers of rock.

Fish

Caught in Time
This spider was trapped in resin, a sticky liquid that dripped down the trunk of an ancient pine tree. The resin hardened into amber.

Skin and Bone
The fossilized foot of this giant extinct bird, called a moa, still has skin attached. You can see how big the foot is by comparing it to a child's hand.

Deep Freeze
This mammoth was frozen in ice at least 12,000 years ago. It may have been trapped in a swamp. When the swamp froze, the mammoth's body was preserved in the ice.

These large footprints belong to an Apatosaurus and are one metre across.

Power from the Past
Did you know that coal and oil are called fossil fuels? They are made from plants or animals that lived and died millions of years ago.

CAVES

Caves are hollows beneath the surface of the Earth. The biggest ones are all found in rock called limestone and some are huge. The world's biggest cave, in Sarawak, is so large that you could fit 800 tennis courts in it. Yet these caves began simply as cracks or holes in the rock that, over thousands of years, were made bigger by rainwater trickling into them and eating them away.

Going Down
Water dripping from the ceiling of a cave leaves behind a mineral called calcite. Very slowly, this grows downwards in an icicle shape that is called a stalactite.

Drip . . .
The rainwater that seeps into the ground is very slightly acid and begins to eat away the limestone.

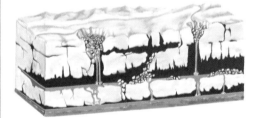

Drip . . .
The rainwater eats through the rock. It widens the cracks into pits, passages and caves.

Drip
Over thousands of years, the passages and caves may join up to make a huge underground system.

Limestone is a very common rock. It is made from the skeletons and shells of tiny sea creatures that died millions of years ago.

The stream disappears underground into a pothole.

This pothole, or tunnel, leads straight down through the rock. It was made by a stream wearing away the rock.

24

Tunnel of Lava

Caves are found in rocks other than limestone. This one is made of lava and is inside a volcano in Hawaii.

Cracks in the rock are widened when rainwater seeps along them.

Limestone pavements are made when the rock is eaten away along joint lines.

Caving In

Sometimes, a cave may be turned into a gorge. This happens when the roof falls in and reveals the caverns and galleries that are hidden underground.

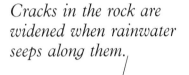

Cliff

Gallery

Cave mouth

Stream

Going Up

Where water drips onto the cave floor, columns of calcite, called stalagmites, grow upwards.

OCEANS

Sun

Earth

Moon

More than two thirds of our planet is covered with water, and oceans and seas make up 71 per cent of the Earth's surface. Beneath the waves lies a fascinating landscape. Much of the ocean floor is a vast plain, but there are also cliffs, trenches and mountain ranges, all larger than any found on dry land.

Pacific Ocean

Atlantic Ocean

Ocean Currents
These show the directions in which water flows.

Cold currents

Warm currents

Ebbing and Flowing
Tides are made by the Sun and Moon pulling on the oceans. When the Sun, Earth and Moon are in a line, there are large spring tides.

Trenches can be deeper than the highest mountains on land.

These underwater islands are called guyots.

Underwater canyons are cut by currents flowing over the seabed like rivers.

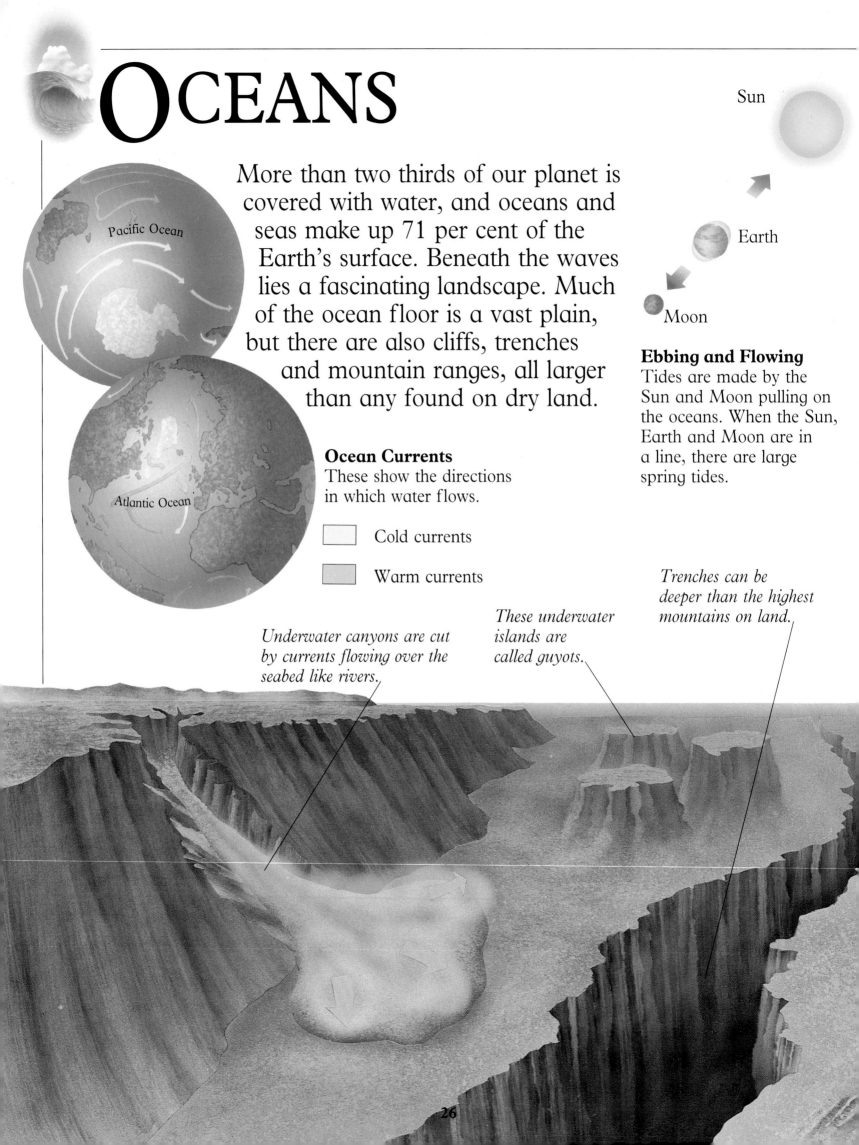

Going . . .
The water inside a wave moves round and round in a circle. It is the wind that drives the wave forwards.

Going . . .
Near the shore, the circular shape of the wave is changed and it becomes squashed.

Gone
The top of the wave becomes unstable. When it hits the beach, it topples and spills over.

Surface

Lighted zone
200 metres

Dark zone
6,000 metres

Deepest zone,
a trench of
11,000 metres

Ocean Currents
The direction in which currents move depends on winds and the Earth's spin. Winds blow the top of the oceans forwards, but the Earth's spin makes the water below go in a spiral.

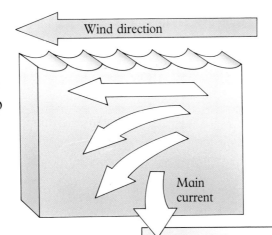

Wind direction

Main current

The Dark Depths
Even in clear water, sunlight cannot reach very far. The oceans become darker and darker the farther down you go, until everything turns inky black.

This island is a volcano that has erupted from the ocean floor.

A long, wide ocean ridge

Water, heated by the hot rocks, shoots back into the sea.

Molten rock rises up, cools and forms new seabed.

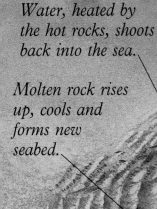

Frozen Worlds
In Antarctica and the Arctic, the oceans freeze. Icebergs break away from glaciers flowing into the water. Only a tiny part of an iceberg is seen above the surface of the ocean.

COASTLINES

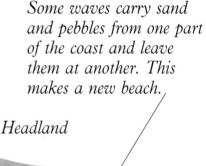

Have you ever built a sand castle and then watched the sea come in, knock it down and flatten it? This is what happens to the coastline, the place where the land and the sea meet. The coastline changes all the time because, every few seconds of every day, waves hit the land and either wear it away or build it up into different shapes.

Some waves carry sand and pebbles from one part of the coast and leave them at another. This makes a new beach.

Headland

Going, Going, Gone
When caves made on both sides of a headland meet, an arch is formed. If the top of the arch falls down, a pillar of rock, called a stack, is left.

An arch

A stack

A cave is made when seawater gets into cracks and holes in a cliff and makes them bigger.

Some beaches are made in bays between headlands where the water is shallow and the waves are weak.

Pounding Away
Waves pound the coastline like a giant hammer until huge chunks of rock are broken off. The chunks are then carried away by the sea and flung against the coastline somewhere else.

From Rocks to Sand
Waves roll rocks and boulders backwards and forwards on the shore. The boulders break into pebbles and then into tiny grains of sand. This change takes hundreds or thousands of years.

Shifting Sands
Dunes are made of sand blown into low hills by the wind.

An estuary is the place where a river flows into the sea.

Sea cliffs are one of the best places to see the different layers of rock.

Mud flats and marshes

Waves can build sand, mud and pebbles into a long strip of new land. It is called a spit.

Living Rock
Coral is found in warm, sunny, shallow seas. It is made by tiny sea creatures that look like flowers. Over thousands of years, their skeletons build up into huge coral reefs and islands.

GLACIERS

A glacier is like a huge river of ice that starts its life as a tiny snowflake. As more and more snow falls and builds up, in time it gets squashed under its own weight and turns into ice.

A glacier moves very slowly downhill. Because it is very heavy, it can push rock along like a bulldozer. It can wear away the sides of mountains, smooth off the jagged bits from rocks and move giant boulders over tens of kilometres.

Mountains

Glaciers begin as huge snowfields.

The snow collects in hollows and turns into ice under its own weight.

Glaciers usually move downhill very slowly, no more than a few centimetres each day.

The ice begins to move and rub away the sides and bottom of the hollow. Little by little, it changes the shape of the land and makes it into a U-shaped valley.

Close-Up View
The pilot in this plane is watching a wall of ice break away from a glacier and begin to crash into the water below.

Ice Power
When the water in this bottle freezes and turns to ice, it takes up more room and breaks the bottle. When the water that makes up the ice of a glacier freezes, it takes up more room and pushes away the rock.

Rubble is carried along by the glacier.

Melted ice flows as streams and rivers inside most glaciers.

Bumps in the rock can be smoothed out by the ice moving downhill.

Rocks carried along by the glacier pile up when the glacier starts to melt and stops pushing them.

The lower end of the glacier is called the 'snout'.

Shaping the Land
When you see a valley like this, you can tell from its U shape that it was once filled with the ice of a glacier.

Out of Place
This giant boulder of hard rock was moved by a glacier and left on soft limestone. Then, most of the limestone was weathered away, leaving a small block under the boulder.

Where a glacier flows into water, chunks of ice break off and float away.

When the glacier melts, it makes new rivers.

RIVERS

Rivers are very powerful, so powerful that the force of the moving water is able to change the shape of the land. As they flow through mountains and over plains, rivers carry away huge amounts of rock, sand and mud. They then dump it somewhere else, usually on riverbanks or in the sea, to make new land.

A river usually begins in mountains or hills. Its water comes from rain or melted snow.

Where the rock is hard, the river makes rapids or waterfalls.

Glacier

Over the Top
When a river tumbles over the edge of a steep cliff or over a hard, rocky ledge, it is called a waterfall. This one is in Brazil, South America.

As the river flows quickly down steep slopes, it wears away the rock to make a V-shaped valley.

Oxbow lake

Sand, mud and gravel are left by the water as sediment.

Round the Bend

When a river reaches flat land, it slows down and begins to flow in large loops. It leaves behind sand, gravel and mud, called deposits. This changes the river's shape and course.

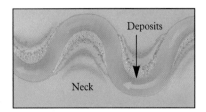

The river leaves deposits on the inside bend and eats away the outer bend.

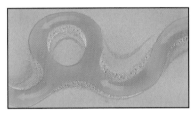

The deposits change the shape of the bend. In time, the neck of the bend narrows and the ends of the neck join up.

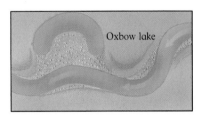

The river leaves behind a loop. It is called an oxbow lake because of its shape.

River Deep

In the USA, the waters of the Colorado River have carved out the largest gorge in the world. It is called the Grand Canyon and it is 1.6 kilometres deep and 350 kilometres long.

River's End

This swampy land is part of the Yukon Delta in Alaska, USA.

A wide bend or meander goes across flat country.

As it reaches the sea, the river divides into small streams to make a delta.

Record Rivers

The longest river in the world is the Nile, in Africa. It is 6,690 kilometres long. The largest delta in the world covers 77,700 square kilometres. It is made by the Ganges and Brahmaputra rivers, in Bangladesh and India.

DESERTS

Did you know that deserts come in many different forms? They can be a sea of rolling sand, a huge area of flat and stony ground or mountainous areas of shattered rock. There are hot deserts and cold deserts. So what do these very different areas have in common? The answer is that they are all very dry and they all get less than 25 centimetres of rain each year. This rain may not fall regularly. Instead, it may all come in a single day and cause a dramatic flash flood.

Sea of Sand
A desert may be hard to live in, but it can be stunning to look at. These dunes are in Saudi Arabia.

Tail dune

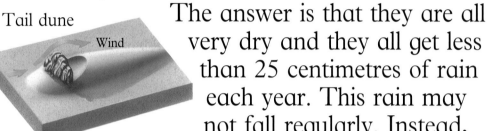

Wind

Barchan dunes

Seif dunes

Star dunes

Wind Power
Wind blows the sand into hills which are called dunes. These have different shapes and names.

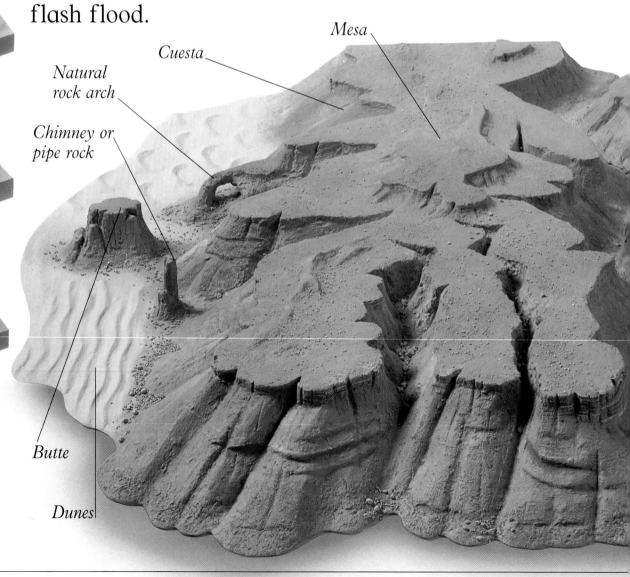

Cuesta

Mesa

Natural rock arch

Chimney or pipe rock

Butte

Dunes

On the Move

Let your hair dryer provide the wind. It blows the sand up the gentle slope of the dune. When the sand gets to the top, it tumbles down the steep slope. As more and more sand is moved from one slope to another, the whole dune moves forwards.

Water Power

The tremendous power of water has made this deep ravine near an oasis in Tunisia.

Heavy rain makes flash floods. These rush over the land, loaded with sand and stones, and cut deep channels in the surface of the desert.

Broken rocks slide downhill and collect in gullies.

Where the rock is hard, ridges will stand out in the landscape.

Shaping the Land

Wind-borne sand blows against the rocks and wears them into beautiful and surprising shapes.

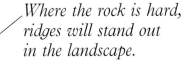

Steep slopes of broken rock

Outwash fan

Hot and Cold

This is one of the Devil's Marbles in the Northern Territory, Australia. The rock's outer layers have started to peel off because of the desert's very hot and very cold temperatures.

THE ATMOSPHERE

Around our planet there is a blanket of gases called the atmosphere. It is so thin that compared to the whole Earth, it is only as thick as the peel of an orange. Yet without this blanket, life on Earth would be impossible. The atmosphere protects us from being roasted by the Sun and frozen by the cold of outer space. It contains the air we need to breathe and makes the rain that provides the water we need to drink.

Most meteors burn up when they enter the atmosphere, so it protects the Earth from their destructive effects.

THERMOSPHERE

MESOSPHERE

The mesosphere is above the stratosphere, 50 to 80 kilometres above the Earth. Shooting stars, or meteors, are seen here.

The troposphere contains most of the gases in the atmosphere and reaches about 11 kilometres above us. This is where the weather occurs.

STRATOSPHERE

Above the troposphere is the stratosphere, which goes from 11 to 50 kilometres above the ground. Aircraft fly here to avoid the weather below.

Rays from the Sun have to pass through the atmosphere to get to the Earth.

TROPOSPHERE

Manned balloon

Ozone is a kind of oxygen that protects the Earth from the harmful rays of the Sun. Without this layer, most living creatures would die.

Mount Everest

Weather balloon

Concorde

The atmosphere lets only half the Sun's rays reach the Earth. Some are absorbed and the rest are reflected back into space.

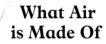

What Air is Made Of

This bunch of balloons shows the amounts of different gases in the atmosphere. The blue balloons are nitrogen, the red ones, oxygen, and the white balloon, all the other gases.

This is a space shuttle. Space shuttles can be used to carry out experiments in space.

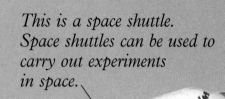

Satellite in orbit

Auroras are bands of flickering, coloured light high in the atmosphere. They are usually seen near the North and South Poles as beautiful, shimmering patterns of green, purple and gold.

The thermosphere is a layer of very thin air found above the mesosphere. It goes from 80 to 480 kilometres above the ground.

Breathless

The higher you go, the less oxygen there is in the air. This is why climbers of very high mountains need to wear oxygen masks.

Breath of Life

We cannot see the air we breathe, but it is vital to us. Without it, we would die. Air is made up of a mixture of gases, including oxygen. The oxygen comes from plants and trees such as the ones shown in this tropical rainforest in Costa Rica.

CLIMATE

What is it like today where you are? Is it cold, hot, snowy, foggy, windy, or a mixture of some of these? Does the weather stay much the same all year round, or does it change with the seasons? Your answers will depend on where you live and on the Sun which plays an important part in making our climate.

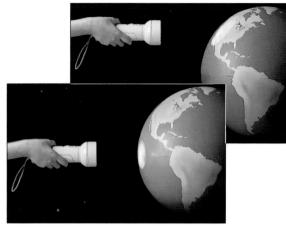

Hot and Cold
Imagine the torch is the Sun. When it shines on the middle of the Earth, it makes a small, hot patch. At the top and bottom the patch spreads out over a bigger area so it heats the land less.

How Hot is It?
Places on the equator are always hot. As you move away from the equator, north or south, it gets colder and colder until you reach the North or South Pole. The bands of colour show you how hot or cold it is in different parts of the world.

Always hot
Hot in summer, warm in winter
Hot in summer, mild in winter
Warm in summer, cold in winter
Cool in summer, cold in winter
Cold all the time

Hottest
Death Valley, USA, is the place where the hottest temperatures have been recorded.

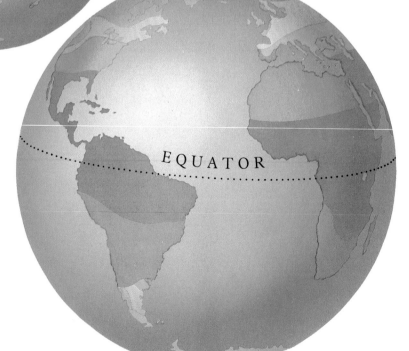

EQUATOR

Coldest
Antarctica is the coldest place on Earth. Snow and ice cover the ground all year.

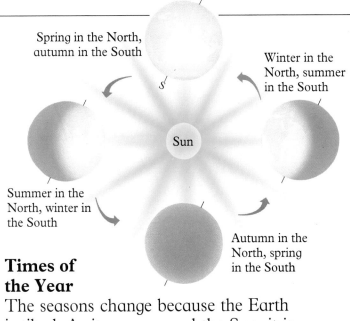

Spring in the North, autumn in the South

N

S

Winter in the North, summer in the South

Sun

Summer in the North, winter in the South

Autumn in the North, spring in the South

Times of the Year

The seasons change because the Earth is tilted. As it goes around the Sun, it is summer in the half near the Sun and winter in the half farthest away.

How Wet is It?

The wettest places on Earth are around the equator, where in some places it rains heavily nearly every day. Generally, it rains less as you travel towards the North or South Pole. Match the colours on the map to the chart and find out how wet or dry each area is.

Heavy rain every month
Light rain every month
Heavy seasonal rain
Light seasonal rain
Hardly ever rains
Snows a lot

Driest

On average, the Atacama Desert is the driest of all the deserts in the world. Only one millimetre of rain falls here each year. The desert is in Chile, in South America.

Wettest

Tutunendo, in Colombia, South America, is the wettest known place. It gets about 11 metres of rain every year.

Disaster in the Making?

Many experts think that the climate is getting warmer. If it warms just a little, and enough of the ice at the Poles melts, low-lying land and cities will be drowned.

CLOUDS

Cirrus clouds are feathery and wispy. They are seen high up in the sky.

16 km

A cloud is made of billions of tiny drops of water so light that they float in the air, but it begins its life as moist air warmed by the Sun. Because warm air is lighter than cold air, it rises in the sky, in just the same way as a hot-air balloon. In a rain cloud, the tiny drops of water join together. They become too large and heavy to float in the air and fall to the ground as rain.

13 km

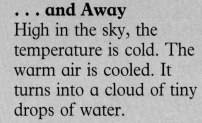

Cirrocumulus

10 km

Altostratus

. . . and Away
High in the sky, the temperature is cold. The warm air is cooled. It turns into a cloud of tiny drops of water.

6 km

Up . . .
The moist air rises up when it is heated by the Sun. The warmed, moist air floats up like bubbles.

Up . . .
For clouds to be made, there must be warm, moist air.

Altocumulus

3 km

Stratocumulus

40

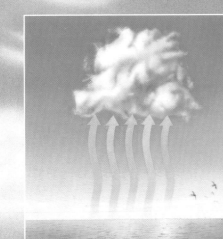

Cumulonimbus

Wet
As warm air flows over seas, lakes and rivers, it picks up water from them.

Wetter
The warm air also takes up water from plants and trees that grow on the land.

Wettest
When the warm, moist air rises, for instance over mountains, it hits cold air and turns into a cloud of tiny water droplets. These come together to make raindrops.

Cumulus clouds are puffy, white masses. They are found between cirrus and stratus clouds. Usually, they bring warm, dry weather.

Stratus clouds look as if they are made up of layers. They are low down in the sky and bring wet, even stormy, weather.

Is it a Bird, is it a Plane?
This strange shape looks like a spacecraft, but it is actually a lenticular cloud.

THUNDER AND LIGHTNING

A bolt of lightning is a giant spark made of static electricity. It is the same sort of electricity that crackles when you run a comb through your hair. Static electricity is made by two things rubbing together. In the case of lightning, it is ice crystals and water drops rubbing against each other in a cloud. Lightning flashes inside a cloud as sheet lightning or from cloud to ground as forked lightning. As it does so, it sends out huge shock waves and makes the noise of thunder.

Static Electricity
When you take off a jumper, your head and the jumper rubbing together sometimes make static electricity.

Thunderclouds are very tall, puffy and dark.

Forked lightning

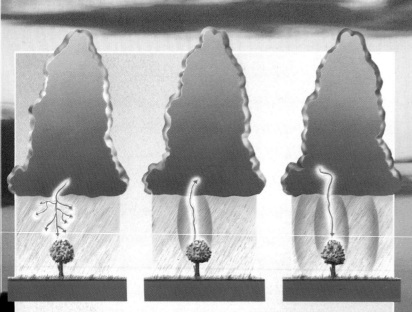

How Lightning Strikes
A flash of lightning is made up of a number of sparks that follow each other so quickly that they look like just one streak. These sparks go backwards and forwards in the cloud or between the cloud and the ground.

Strange Behaviour
Ball lightning looks like a round fireball and may be white, red, yellow or blue. It tends to get into buildings through chimneys and escape under doors.

Direct Hit
Fork lightning finds the quickest, easiest way to the ground. This is why trees and tall buildings are in such danger of being struck.

As a lightning bolt flashes through the air, the air around becomes five times as hot as the surface of the Sun.

The core of a flash of lightning may be as thin as one centimetre.

Full of Energy
A bolt of lightning has enough energy in it to power a small town for a year.

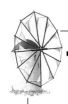

WIND

Wind is air that is moving around. You can't see it, but you can feel it, and you can see what it does. Wind can be as gentle as a breeze that ruffles your hair or as violent as a hurricane – also known as a cyclone – that rips up trees and buildings and flattens all in its path.

Pointing into the Wind

Weather vanes swing around so that the front points into the wind, showing you the direction from which the wind is blowing.

Why the Winds Blow

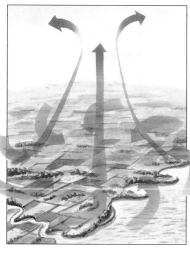

The winds are made by air rising or falling. When air is warmed by the Sun, it rises. Cool air is then drawn in to take the place of the warm air. When air is cool, it is heavy and sinks down, moving out in sweeping curves when it reaches the surface of the Earth.

In a Spin

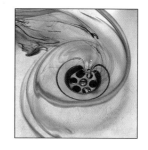

Water spins down a plughole in a strong swirl with a hole in the middle. It goes down in a spin because the Earth is spinning. A hurricane does the same thing, only upwards.

What Happens in a Hurricane

The top of the cloud is icy.

Clouds spread out at the top.

The hurricane sucks in cool air, which takes the place of the hot air.

At the centre of the spiral is a calm spot called the eye.

Torrential rains fall around the eye.

Picking up Speed

The Beaufort Scale tells you how fast a wind is blowing and how strong it is. It is based on the effect the wind has on such things as trees and houses. The strength of the wind is measured in forces from 0 to 12.

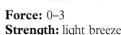

Force: 0–3
Strength: light breeze
Speed: 4–24 km/h

Weather Warning

These satellite photos from space show how a hurricane builds up. It starts where storms over the sea come together in a big, powerful swirl.

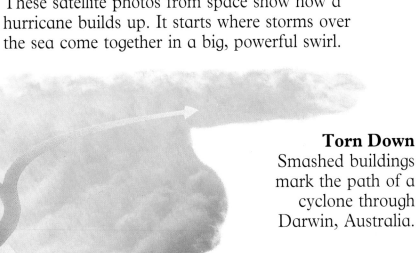

Torn Down

Smashed buildings mark the path of a cyclone through Darwin, Australia.

Some hurricanes may be 800 km across.

Hot air rises and spirals up around the eye.

Destructive Force

Tornadoes are whirling funnels of wind that suck trees, cars and buildings into the air like a giant vacuum cleaner and then throw them to the ground.

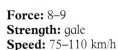
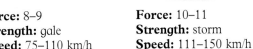

Force: 4–5
Strength: moderate wind
Speed: 25–46 km/h

Force: 6–7
Strength: strong wind
Speed: 47–74 km/h

Force: 8–9
Strength: gale
Speed: 75–110 km/h

Force: 10–11
Strength: storm
Speed: 111–150 km/h

Force: 12
Strength: hurricane
Speed: above 150 km/h

TAKING CARE OF THE EARTH

Earth is an incredible place, teeming with animals, insects, fish, birds, plants and people. Like a Noah's Ark in space, it provides a home for all. It gives us shelter, warmth, food, water and the air we breathe.

Like Noah's boat, our ark needs looking after. Its air, oceans and rain need to be cleaned up, its forests saved and its soil protected from harmful chemicals. It is a big task, but we Earthlings can do it.

Saving the Seas
Cleaning up the pollution in our seas and oceans will help save the world's sea creatures from becoming extinct.

Trees of Life
If we stop destroying the tropical rainforests, millions of species of birds, animals, insects and plants will keep their homes.

Driving Force
In the future, cars may run on solar power, using energy from the Sun. Other alternatives to petrol include fuels that are made from plants such as sugar cane.

Cleaning the Air
Cutting down on the amount of chemicals pumped out by factories and car exhaust pipes will improve the quality of the air we breathe.

Living Space
Our planet is home to billions of people. We need to make sure that it is not swamped by sheer weight of numbers.

How You Can Help
Recycle bottles, cans, paper and aluminium foil.
Avoid using plastic packaging.
Save energy by switching off lights when they are not needed.
When possible, use paper that has been recycled.

Back from the Brink
If we protect wildlife from being hunted and preserve the places it lives in, animals, such as this leopard, will be saved from extinction.

GLOSSARY

Atmosphere A blanket of gases that surrounds a planet or moon.

Butte A small, flat-topped hill found in deserts.

Chimney rock Hard rock in a desert that has been worn into a pinnacle.

Climate The average weather in an area.

Coastline The place where the land and the sea meet.

Continent One of seven large areas of land on Earth.

Coral reef A mass of coral, the top of which is very near the sea's surface.

Cuesta A step of hard rock found in deserts.

Current Movement in a particular direction by sea or river water.

Delta A mass of sand, mud and rock fragments formed at a river's mouth.

Desert Any place where less than 25 centimetres of rain falls a year.

Dune A heap of sand blown into a hill by wind.

Earthquake Sudden movements in the Earth's crust that cause violent shaking.

Equator An imaginary line around the Earth's middle.

Estuary The place where a river goes into the sea.

Flash flood A sudden, violent flood in a desert.

Focus The place under the Earth where an earthquake starts.

Fossil Animal or plant remains that have been preserved in rock.

Galaxy A huge 'island' of stars in space.

Glacier A mass of ice moving slowly down a mountain.

Globe A sphere that has a map of the world drawn on it.

Gorge A deep, narrow valley cut by a river.

Hurricane A strong wind that forms over seas in tropical areas.

Lava Red-hot, melted rock that erupts from a volcano onto the Earth's surface.

Magma Melted rock under the Earth's surface.

Mantle The layer of the Earth below the crust.

Mercalli Scale A way of measuring how much the surface of the Earth shakes during an earthquake.

Mesa A large, flat-topped, steep-sided area of land in a desert.

Moon A ball of rock in space that goes around a planet.

Ocean A huge sea.

Planet A large round object that orbits a star.

Satellite A moon or other object in space that goes around a planet or star.

Season A time of the year with a special climate.

Sediment Sand, mud and gravel moved from one place to another by wind, water or ice.

Spit A new piece of land made of sand, mud and pebbles built by the waves.

Stack A rock pillar left standing in coastal waters when the top of an arch falls in.

Tide The regular rising and falling of the sea.

Tornado A whirling funnel of wind.

U-shaped valley The channel worn away by a glacier moving downhill.

V-shaped valley The channel worn away by a river as it flows downhill.

Volcano The place where hot, liquid rock breaks through the Earth's crust.

Weathering The breaking up of rocks by wind, rain and ice.

Acknowledgments

Photography: Tina Chambers, Geoff Dann, Steve Gorton, James Stevenson.

Illustrations: Jim Channell, Roy Flooks, Mick Gillah, Keith Hume.

Models: Donks Models.

Thanks to: H. Samuel Ltd., Truly Scrumptious Child Model Agency.

Picture credits

Ancient Art & Architecture Collection: 22; **Ardea:** François Gohier 46r, Clem Haagner 11b, 47b, D. Parer & E. Parer-Cook 11t; **Biofotos:** Heather Angel 31cr, Bryn Campbell 27, Brian Rogers 31cra; **Bruce Coleman:** Stephen J. Kraseman 47tl; **Frank Lane Picture Agency:** Australian Information Service 45tr, Ray Bird 43r, R. Jennings 43l, S. McCutcheon 30clb; **G.S.F. Picture Library:** 3, 14, 15, 25tr; **Rafn Hafnfjord:** 13; **Robert Harding Picture Library:** 25tl, 45b; **Image Bank:** James H. Carmichael 37; **Japan Meteorological Agency/National Meteorological Library, Bracknell:** back cover, 45tl(1-5); **Mountain Camera:** John Cleare 36; **NASA:** 6t & b; **NHPA:** A.N.T./Grant Dixon 39t, G.I. Bernard 46l; **Oxford Scientific Films:** Doug Allen 41, Stuart Bebb 18l, Martyn Colbeck 35c, Warren Faidley 42/43, Terry Middleton 25b; **Dr. Chris Pellant:** 28; **Pictor:** 1, 21, 33t; 40; **Planet Earth Pictures:** Rob Beighton 38c, G. Deichmann/Transglobe 35b, Hans Christian Heap 34, back cover, John Lythgoe 18r, Mike Potts 33b, K. Puttock 38b; **Science Photo Library:** ESA front cover, 4tl, 8tl, Geosphere Project, Santa Monica/Tom Van Sant 8cr, 9cl, Maptec International 8tr, NASA 8bl, 9tl & tr, 38t, National Snow & Ice Data Center 9cr, Claude Nuridsany & Marie Perennou 30tl, cla & bl, 31tr & br, David Parker 16, Sheila Terry 19r; **South American Pictures:** Tony Morrison 39b; **John Massey Stewart:** 23; **ZEFA:** 47tr, ALLSTOCK/W. McIntyre 19l, ALLSTOCK/Art Wolfe endpapers, A.P.L. 29b, DAMM 32, Knight & Hunt 35t, Rossenbach 29t.

t – **top**	l – **left**	a – **above**	cb – **centre below**
b – **bottom**	r – **right**	c – **centre**	clb – **centre left below** crb – **centre right below**

INDEX

A

Allosaurus 22
amber 23
Antarctica 27, 38
Apatosaurus 22, 23
Arctic 27
ash 14, 15
asteroid 6
astronaut 8
atmosphere 36–37, 48
auroras 37

B

ball lightning 43
beach 28
Beaufort Scale 44–45
block mountain 11
butte 34, 48

C

calcite 20, 24, 25
canyons 26
caves 24–25, 28
chimney rock 34, 48
cliffs 26
climate 38–39, 48
clouds 40–41
  cirrus 40, 41
  cumulus 41
  stratus 41
coal 23
coastlines 28–29, 48
comet 6
conglomerate 18
continents 8, 9, 11, 12, 13, 48
coral 29, 48
core 10
crater 14
crust, Earth's 10–11, 12, 14, 17, 18, 19
crystals 20
cuesta 34, 48
currents 26, 27, 48

D

delta 33, 48
deposits 33
deserts 34–35, 39, 48
diamond 20, 21
dinosaur 22, 23
downfold 10

dunes 29, 34, 35, 48
  barchan 34
  seif 34
  star 34
  tail 34

E

Earth 6, 7, 8, 9, 12, 13, 24
earthquakes 12, 13, 16–17, 48
electricity 42
epicentre 17
Equator 38, 39, 48
estuary 29, 48

F

fault 10, 16
feldspar 20
focus 17, 48
fork lightning 43
fossils 22–23, 48

G

galaxy 6, 48
gems 21
glaciers 27, 30–31, 32, 48
globe 13, 48
gold 21
gorge 25, 33
granite 19, 20
gypsum 20, 21

H

headland 28
hematite 20
hot springs 14
hurricane 44, 45, 48

I

icebergs 27
igneous rocks 18, 19
intensity 17
iron ore 20
islands 26, 27

J

Jupiter 6, 7

L

lava 12, 14, 15, 18, 25, 48
lightning 42–43
limestone 18, 24, 25

M

magma 15, 18, 19, 48
mammoth 23
mantle 10, 18, 48
map 9

marble 19
Mars 6, 7
marsh 29
meander 33
Mercalli Scale 17, 48
Mercury 6, 7
mercury 20
mesa 34, 48
mesosphere 36
metals 20, 21
metamorphic rocks 18, 19
meteor 36
mica 20
Milky Way 6
minerals 20–21, 24
Moa 23
Mohs Scale 20
Moon 6, 48
mountains 10, 12, 18, 19, 32
mud flats 29

N

Neptune 7
nitrogen 37
North Pole 8, 38, 39

O

obsidian 19
oceans 8, 9, 26–27, 46, 48
oil 23
orbit 6
ores 20
outwash fan 35
overfold 10
oxbow lake 32, 33
oxygen 36, 37
ozone 36

P

pebbles 28, 29
pipe rock 34
planets 6, 7, 48
plate 12–13, 17
Pluto 7
pollution 46
Pompeii 22
pothole 24

Q

quartz 20, 21

R

rainforests 37, 46
rainwater 24, 25
ravine 35
recycling 47
red sandstone 18

ridge 27
rivers 18, 32–33
rocks 18–19, 20

S

sand 28, 29, 34, 35
sapphire 21
Saturn 7
sea 8, 18, 28, 29, 46
seasons 39, 48
sediment 32, 48
sedimentary rocks 18, 19
shockwaves 17
silver 21
solar power 46
Solar System 6
South Pole 8, 38, 39
space 6, 7, 8, 9
spit 29, 48
stalactites 24
stalagmites 25
stratosphere 36
Sun 6, 7, 46

T

thermosphere 36, 37
thunder 42–43
tides 26, 48
tornado 45, 48
troposphere 36
tsunami 16, 17

U

universe 6
upfold 10
Uranus 7

V

valley
  rift 11
  U-shaped 30, 31, 48
  V-shaped 32, 48
Venus 6, 7
Vesuvius 22
volcanoes 12, 14–15, 18, 19, 27, 48

W

waterfall 32
waves 26, 28, 29
weathering 18, 19, 48
weather vane 44
winds 18, 19, 44–45